CONFUCIUS IN MY CUBICLE

Practical Wisdom for the Leader in All of Us

CATHY PERME

Wisdom Editions

Minneapolis

Wisdom
Editions
Minneapolis

FIRST EDITION DECEMBER2017
CONFUCIUS IN MY CUBICLE, Copyright © 2017 by Cathy Perme
All rights reserved.

Excerpt(s) from THE PARADOX OF SUCCESS: WHEN WINNING AT WORK MEANS LOSING AT LIFE by John R. O'Neil, copyright © 1993 by John O'Neil. Used by permission of Tarcher, an imprint of Penguin Publishing Group, a division of Penguin Random House LLC. All rights reserved.

Confucius quotes: Translation, introduction, and annotation © copyright 2014 by David Hinton, from Analects. Reprinted by permission of Counterpoint.

Printed in the United States of America.
10 9 8 7 6 5 4 3 2 1

Cover and interior design: Gary Lindberg

ISBN: 978-1-939548-81-8

CONFUCIUS IN MY CUBICLE

Practical Wisdom for the
Leader in All of Us

CATHY PERME

For my daughter Lucy, the light of my life,
who was born in the Land of Confucius.

TABLE OF CONTENTS

Part 3: Managing Change (Yours!)   63

Part 4: Finding Balance   85

References   107

Endnotes   111

About the Author   113

Acknowledgements

This first book has been a long time coming! I would like to thank my current and former book coaches, Royce Holladay and Ian Leask, for their encouragement and insights. I would also like to thank Anne Knapp and Glenda Eoyang, personal and professional colleagues who have been invaluable and frequent collaborators with me in my work. I have learned much from each of them, which is reflected in this book.

Finally, I would like to thank my clients. All gave me the opportunity to witness leadership in action, for better or worse, and trusted me to be a partner in their success.

FOREWORD

This is not your typical leadership book. This book is short, to the point, and doesn't add filler. It is not meant to be read cover to cover (although you could if you wanted.) Instead it is meant for you to flip through and read what grabs your attention, relevant for you at that moment. You see, I wrote the kind of book that I like to read!

While the world has changed significantly since Confucius lived 2500 years ago, I marvel at how much of his teaching still resonates. His philosophy about what it means to be a good leader and how to be human—and humane with one another—is still sorely needed. In this book, you will find essays and stories that weave this philosophy into modern leadership ideas.

But there is something that Confucius never had to deal with—finding balance between work and life. Today we generally have much more free-dom between men and women and our societal roles. Many of us take on significant responsibilities for both work and family. In addition, today's technol-ogy can tether us to work 24 hours a day, 7 days a week, 365 days a year—draining focus and attention from things that matter. As a result, you will also find essays that Confucius would have never conceived.

These essays reflect lessons from my experi-ence with clients and my own life as a business own-er, consultant, mother, daughter, wife, friend, and mentor. Each essay is short and will provide enough background and information to help you think about something differently. It will also give you advice about how to put those ideas into practice.

As Confucius said, "If you can revive the an-cient and use it to understand the modern, then you're worthy to be a teacher" (2.11). I aspire to this goal, and I hope you enjoy this book!

Who Was Confucius, and Why Does He Matter Today?

To honor my daughter's Chinese heritage, I decided to learn about Confucius' life and teachings. After some reading and research, I've come to think of him as the original consultant! Why? He traveled from kingdom to kingdom (business to business), advised their courts (leadership teams), facilitated group discussions (about values and change), and coached people (through questioning them) to be better leaders.

Confucius lived at a time of great social and political upheaval, with kingdoms fighting kingdoms. A primary focus for him was to reduce chaos because he believed if leaders could help reduce chaos, it would create a "virtuous circle," with people becoming more likely to invest in their families and livelihoods, thereby bringing about greater calm and prosperity.

What I find most amazing is that advice given 2,500 years ago is still so relevant, even with the ever-increasing speed and complexity of our lives. His challenge (for leaders to be humane and focus on the common good, for education to lift society, and for everyone to perform their roles well) provides a common-sense approach to our problems today as well.

With sincere apologies to Chinese philosophers for any oversimplifications, here are some big Confucian ideas I've found useful in my life as an American mom and businesswoman.

- **Leadership is about wisdom and compassion.** Approximately 100 years before Socrates and 500 years before Jesus of Nazareth, Confucius uttered what we know today as the Golden Rule—treating others the way you would want to be treated. Most often, this teaching was aimed at leaders, the warlords who often had little regard for their subjects. To Confucius, leaders had great responsibility to treat their people with respect and care, and they had a moral imperative to promote the common good.

- **Nobility is achieved through education and moral behavior.** In an age when leaders were thought to be embodiments of gods, and when nobility was a birthright, Confucius shook up the old order. He said nobility was achieved through education and moral behavior, leadership could be learned, and that even a peasant could be a noble man.

- **Do your job, and do it well.** If you conclude that Confucius was tough on leaders (he was), you also should know he was tough on everyone. He did not coddle whiners or underachievers. He expected everyone to perform their roles to the best of their abilities. Having a low-level or boring job did not absolve you of this requirement because he was convinced that every job or role has value in a well-functioning society.

Confucius' teachings were brought to life for me while consulting with the custodial services department of a large urban school district. Routinely called "janitors," they clean schools and keep them in good working order. They are often hampered by outdated equipment, time constraints, and a challenging customer base. (Imagine the stress of constantly cleaning up after your kids, but for 300 to 2,000 of them at a time!) The work is not pretty, and it is hard. These workers are on the low end of the pecking order for attention, respect, and funding.

And yet… and yet… the people I worked with had an incredible sense of pride and ownership in the work they did, and they saw themselves as an integral part of their school teams. In my work with them, a team of volunteers from the group took on the challenging work of redesigning outdated processes to improve productivity, teamwork, and results. It was not easy nor popular work. I doubt any of the custodians who joined this effort set out to be leaders, but they were, having stepped up to co-create important changes for the common good.

I was honored to work with such a thoughtful and courageous group. And I think Confucius would have been proud.

PART 1:
TAKING THE LEAD

For Confucius, leadership meant being of service, having integrity, and taking care of people as you went along. These ideas were central to his teaching, and they were how he *defined* nobility—a notion that challenged the very foundation of Chinese society at the time.

> *While the noble-minded cherish integrity, little people cherish territory. And while the noble-minded cherish laws, little people cherish privilege. (1.11)*

Confucius challenges each of us to lead from our own position in society or our organizations—in service to others, with integrity, honesty, and care. This does not mean rolling over and playing dead when politics heat up; it does mean standing up to and for our leaders with honesty, integrity, and care.

> *Don't worry if you have no position; worry about making yourself worthy of one. Don't worry if you aren't known and admired: devote yourself to a life that deserves admiration. (1.14)*

> *To serve first, and let the rewards follow as they will—is that not exalting integrity? To attack evil itself, not the evil person—is that not reforming depravity? To endanger yourself and your family, all in a morning's blind rage—is that not delusion? (12.21)*

Leadership also means recognizing that we have free will, and we will follow leaders we trust will care for us.

> *Vast armies can be robbed of their commander, but even the simplest people cannot be robbed of their free will. (9.26)*

> *One day the stables burned down. When he returned from court, the Master asked: Was anyone hurt?" He did not ask about the horses. (10.11)*

The essays that follow carry the spirit of Confucius as we attempt to lead through the chaotic landscape of today's modern world, although I dare say Confucius might have resonated with these as well!

Cathy Perme

Front Line Leadership

We seem to be grappling with a world that is shifting so fast it is hard to figure out which way to go—terrorism, threats, recessions, global changes. Never has the call for "leadership" seemed so urgent—and welcomed so heartily when it appears.

However, leadership is not reserved for one or a few. That is a myth we have held for the last centuries, when the word "leadership" was first used to describe a political appointment. The word "lead" is derived from an Old English word that means "a course, a way, or a journey" and is connected to another word we use today—"load" --which is something we carry (Webster's New World College Dictionary 4th Edition, 1999, p. 841). *So, the real meaning of leadership is to bring something on a journey, with the implication we deliver it intact.*

Unfortunately, in today's world, no business or nation can rely on a single set of individuals at the top to know about everything that is happening, nor can we rely on them to decide quickly, accurately, and fairly what to do about it. That might have worked in the slower-paced days of the last several centuries, but not now and not into the future.

We each need to step into the leadership journey, taking responsibility for bringing others and ourselves into the future intact. So, what is our job, if we cannot delegate all this upward to presidents, executives, and CEO's?

First, it is our job to *accept and face today's reality* head on—no wishing, no whining, no denying, and no panicking. Everyone needs to be part of constantly gathering and sharing information about customers, competitors, markets, products, and processes. Collaboration and teamwork are key to make sense of this data and to know where to focus attention.

Second, it is our job to *engage in a vision for the future that goes beyond today's fear*. Although it is cliché to say people are our primary resource— in great companies and countries that is true. Every single person takes a leadership role within his or her own sphere of influence. They share the vision and goals, they understand their role, and they act.

Third, it is our job to *keep ourselves fresh, open-minded, creative, and learning*. Lifelong learning, new opportunities, personal feedback, and self-reflection are essential ingredients to personal development and long-term employability. Unless we do this, we will stagnate and find change harder and harder.

Fourth, it is our job to *live in concert with our values*. That means *knowing* what our personal values are, and ensuring our values align with the company for whom we work. (There is absolutely no joy in working for a company whose values conflict with those we hold dear!) It also means having the courage to stand up for our personal and national values when they seem threatened or compromised. That is called integrity.

Finally, it is our job to *respect the leadership of others and help them lead, too*. That means we realize we may have differences of opinion or different ways of doing things. And it means, even where we disagree, we must support each other, and challenge each other in *helpful* ways so everyone reaches the future together, intact!

Cathy Perme

The Anatomy of a Change Agent

What makes a change agent different from someone who just raises hell and makes life difficult for
everyone else? The difference lies in their sense of
responsibility for the change itself and their *care* for
the people who must live with the change.

I participated in an intensive research and study
group on non-violent systems change that drove this
message home. Within our small group in Bandera,
Texas, change agents from Northern Ireland, Albania
and the Balkans, South Africa, and the U.S., talked
about lessons learned from their work in non-vi-
olence. Some held positions of power, some were
community activists, and some simply found themselves in situations they could not ignore. Our con-
versations were intense, real, and immediate. Here
is what I learned about change agents in the midst of
change:

- **Real change agents have often had a "watershed moment" when they recognized, with keen perception, the entirety of a situation and what they could do to influence it.** One of our group, a Protestant minister from Northern Ireland, once bore the casket of a young Catholic boy killed by extremists. His courage at that moment helped to avert further retaliation and bloodshed in his own community.

- **Real change agents are skilled individuals who are comfortable with themselves.** They are clear about their values; they understand their own motivations; they are confident in their own skills; and they know how to build coalitions and ask for help. They may be a product of their history, but they are neither blinded nor possessed by it.

- **Real change agents are willing to submit their egos to a larger goal.** It was often not easy for the three folks from Northern Ireland who represented different interests to be in the same room together. But they had a common goal—sustaining peace—and they were firmly dedicated to it.

Nelson Mandela listed three decisions that set expectations for this shift. "Before we started negotiations with the enemy, we made the following three decisions:

1. We decided from our work and from our struggle, that people must win and not one political party.

2. There are good people in all communities—and political parties—not just the ANC.

3. That smaller parties joining our government will be heard and their views given due importance."

Nelson Mandela
Former President of South Africa
March 1997

Real change agents build energy and consensus, and do not divide and conquer. The allure of power politics is overwhelming and can often produce short-term results. Each of these change agents knew long term, systemic change came from the people whose lives were affected by it. Their focus was on ways to build trust, dialog, and movement to help people let go of perceptions and beliefs that limit their future.

There are real change agents working every day in our organizations and communities. Being a change agent is not about personality. It's not about leadership style. It *is* about awareness, conviction, humanity, and courage. It is a far cry from just raising hell.

THE ANATOMY OF A CHANGE AGENT

- A **CLEAR MIND** that is not cluttered with unresolved issues or unexamined motives

- **EYES** that see beyond today

- **EARS** that listen to other points of view

- A **NOSE** that senses opportunities and timing

- A **MOUTH** that speaks out with honesty and respect

- A **HEART** that feels others' pain and responds with compassion

- A **FIRE IN THE BELLY**, a sense of passion and responsibility that makes one want to rise each morning

- **SKILLFUL HANDS** that do scut work as well as strategy

- **LIGHT FEET** that move swiftly when the timing is right

- The **SOUL OF A WARRIOR**, with a deep sense of honor, perseverance, and patience, along with the willingness to act decisively

DEALING WITH SCARY TIMES

牛

Figure 1. Chinese character for Ox (2004)

In scary times—wars, disasters, terrorism, political unrest—the easiest thing to do is to crawl into a shell and stay there until (we hope) everything sorts itself out. Lucky for us, the Chinese sign of Ox carries some excellent advice about how to approach times like these. The Ox is a symbol of strength, focus, and determination. It promises prosperity through hard work and sustained effort. It is also an animal that works in teams and nourishes the community in which it lives. So, what does the Ox suggest for the leader in all of us during scary times?

- **Focus**—*on the future.*

  Don't make the mistake of making only short-term decisions to conserve your resources (the turtle approach) without refocusing for a new, and probably different, future. The Ox guides us to consider the consequences of decisions for both the short-term *and* the long term and to balance the needs of both.

- **Invest**—*by "plowing the ground for the future."*

  Now is the time to invest in building new skills, developing capacity, and expanding networks to be ready for a different future. Don't have a lot of money? You can still invest by volunteering time and effort to provide new learning opportunities, community visibility, and expanded networks.

- **Team up**—*and care for the people around you.*

  More than ever, it is important to build partnerships and teamwork across organizations and industries to identify and shape new opportunities for the future. It is also important to care for people (employees, customers, community, vendors, etc.) who make your business a success. Now is the time to be generous with others.

- **Work hard**—*because that's what it will take*.

Remember oxen teams often work 12-14 hours a day when planting and harvesting. This is no time to slack off.

- **Stay positive**—*your reputation depends on it*.

Keep a positive attitude and get help if you feel down. Your attitude is your strength. Remember the Chinese saying, "The times produce their heroes."

Cathy Perme

LEADING IN CHAOTIC TIMES

Does this sound familiar? You are sitting in your office, taking a brief break in a day filled with back-to-back meetings. There are stacks of "to read" folders on your desk. Your smartphone dings incessantly signaling incoming messages and you have half a dozen callbacks to make before going home. Just a typical day at the office ...

... At the same time, the market has taken a turn and revenue is down across the company. To keep expenses in line, you've had to lay-off staff and reduce investments. Morale is low. Nevertheless, you are expected to strengthen your products, services, and customer relationships, and to come out ready to be stronger than ever.

As a leader, what do you do? Every time you think you have a plan, the ground shifts. The more you try to predict what will happen, the less things happen the way you expect. How can you lead effectively if you can't control anything? Based on what we know about turbulent systems, the best things you can do now are:

1. **Confront reality** - You are in a new, evolving landscape. The future is uncertain and there are lots of divergent opinions about what to do. The old notions that "you can plan and control your environment" simply don't apply. Accept this and begin to adopt new leadership techniques.

2. **Look for patterns** - Ask questions and engage employees, customers, and others in discussions about what they see happening and why. Look for patterns that help you understand the forces, direction, and pace of change.

3. **Create focus** - Based on what you've learned, define the boundaries of the new landscape. Clarify objectives (the more turbulent the environment, the more short-term and tangible the objectives need to be). Identify the variables that matter and set "simple rules" ("Simple Rules", 2016) for how you want people to behave.

What are Simple Rules?[2]

One of the most useful concepts to come out of complex systems theory is the concept of "simple rules." Simple rules are short, concrete guides for informing action to create patterns in a system. They are an excellent way to inform individual and group behavior in rapidly changing environments.

- To work, "simple rules" must be short, direct, and few. They must prescribe specific actions or behaviors and address the most important variables in the system.

- Take white-water rafting. In a churning river, things are moving too fast for a paddler to analyze and plan each action. He or she must rely on a few simple rules to survive:

- Paddle faster than the current (which enables steering), and

- Shoot for the "V" (usually a path in the water between the rocks).

4. **Empower people to "go!"** - Direct your employees to focus on the variables that matter; empower them to act and make decisions based on the "simple rules." Rely on real-time

information, rather than tight supervision, to guide their efforts.

5. **Structure robust feedback loops** - Information is oxygen in rapidly changing environments. Deploy regular communication mechanisms that continually loop information between you, your employees, and your customers: get people together, encourage exchanges, report performance, and solicit feedback. Use the information to inform action.

At some point, you may find things do settle down again (i.e. become more certain and you can all agree on what to do), and you have moved back into more predictable space, where you can plan and control. In the chaotic landscape however, as in white water, you need to paddle fast and shoot for the "V!"

TEACHING OLD DOGS NEW TRICKS

There is an old saying "you can't teach an old dog new tricks." As an "old dog" myself, I beg to differ. I have seen "old dogs" not only learn "new tricks," but *transform* those tricks into a new reality that is more productive, more effective, more creative, and more enjoyable.

"Old dogs" are not so much defined by age as by mastery level. Malcolm Gladwell (2011), in his book *Outliers: The Story of Success*, said "10,000 hours of practice are required to achieve the level of mastery associated with being a world-class expert–in anything" (p. 40). Therefore, if a person spends 10,000 hours working in a specific area or job (akin to about 20 hours per week for 10 years) they have probably achieved a certain level of mastery in that area.

As a result, "old dogs" have figured out how to employ their skills effectively and efficiently based on what is under their control. And that is the rub! So much of life and work is not controllable, and achieving mastery in any specific area can provide a false sense of security. When the job or environment changes, however, "old dogs" may be forced to learn new skills that challenge their sense of mastery.

But when "old dogs" can see the big picture and be involved in adapting their skills to a *new* reality, they can literally transform it AND themselves in the process. What kind of leadership helps "old dogs" go beyond new tricks to create new realities?   It is leadership that:

- Helps them see the big picture and clarify the need. One of my favorite reference points is the change formula coined by Richard Beckhard and Reuben Harris (1987), organizational development pioneers– "DxVxF>R":

  o "D" = Dissatisfaction with today

  o "V" = Vision for the future

  o "F" = First Steps to get there

  The greater the shared understanding of D, V, and F, the greater the potential for overcoming "R," or resistance to change.   If D, V, or F is low or missing however, resistance will be difficult to overcome.

- Listens intensively to what they say and invites them to help in developing the solution.

- Does not discount what they already do well, but helps them build on that foundation. "Old dogs" have pride in their work, and a challenge to how they do things may be construed as a challenge to their pride.

- "Shows" them versus "tells" them what the new reality will look like.

- Provides plenty of time to learn new skills and practice in a supportive environment.

A great example of this is the facilities maintenance department of a large urban school district, which transformed their processes to be more effective. Intensive listening was key. More than half of the tradespeople were involved in shaping new systems and processes. In doing so, they honored their own mastery and built a strong foundation for the future.

Staffed by 56 skilled tradespeople in 11 different trades and represented by 14 different unions, this department was under the gun to improve their productivity and reduce their backlog of repairs for an aging infrastructure.

- A time study showed almost half their time was spent in "white space"—i.e. unproductive time spent deciphering paperwork, locating information, and chasing down parts.

- Despite their alleged "fat fingers," these folks embraced a new software technology system that streamlined internal processes and improved communications with customers and each other. It gives them real-time access to inventory and project information so they can actually fix things, not just plan to fix them.

- In the process of learning these new tricks, not only did they reduce their "white space," they established a new culture of teamwork, transparency, and customer service that had been missing in the past.

The reality is that **all the above** can apply to "new dogs" as well, so the bottom line is that what "old dogs" need from their leaders in terms of change is simply… good leadership from clarity, support, and a constructive and appreciative approach.

ORGANIZATIONAL CULTURE:
WHAT EVERYONE NEEDS TO KNOW

Who owns the culture of a company? If you're a leader who thinks <u>you</u> do … think again. There's more to the culture picture, and some surprising news about which cultures can be predictors of organizational success.

CULTURE IS ABOUT UNDERLYING ASSUMPTIONS

According to Edgar Schein, who was the first person to coin the phrase "organizational culture" in the mid-1960's, culture is framed by what we assume to be true (assumptions and beliefs) about our organization and our environment. It is also unconscious, it is learned, and it is reinforced when problems can be solved repeatedly with the same approach.

Let's take the example of high-tech companies, which started in the boom times of the 1990's and have been up and down since then. What do you think are their assumptions about themselves and their environment? Doesn't the future seem unlimited? Aren't they like the cowboys of the last great frontier—technology? Let's think about how their culture is learned and reinforced. Remember all those articles about pinball games in the break rooms, free lattes, and the fun and crazy company meetings? And what about when they needed more capital—wasn't it readily available?

Culture Eventually Calcifies

In the early years of an organization, the entrepreneur or leader does influence the culture greatly—because what gets implemented is that person's perspective on the environment and the business fit. If the perspective is out of touch, the company probably goes out of business. However, if the company survives—and even thrives—because of this perspective, culture has begun to take root.

In the beginning, culture is passed on orally and with much passion, as in "this is how we do things around here." Eventually, however, organizations grow up, and their perspectives about how to operate in their worlds become embedded through policies and procedures, processes, hiring, promotion, and reward structures.

At some point, the organizational culture becomes bigger than its leaders, and it molds leaders to fit culture, instead of vice-versa. Leaders who try to change problems embedded in the culture have an uphill battle, and many are caught in a death grip. (Think about our efforts to reform government and public schools—when what we are really dealing with is 100+ years of assumptions based on outmoded models of civil service and education!)

Adaptability is Key

Based on long-standing research[3], cultures most likely to sustain high performance over time displayed two key descriptors. They are constructive, and they facilitate the adoption of strategies and practices to respond continuously to changing markets and new competitive environments.

These cultures support the organization's immediate strategy and business context, develop good teamwork and internal cooperation, look forward, and guide positive change. Key characteristics of these cultures are that they:

- Maintain a fit between the culture and the business context

- Ensure active support between and among members of the organization

- Focus on identifying problems and finding workable solutions

- Reflect confidence among all members of an organization

- Nurture trust

- Support risk taking

- Act proactively

Organizations with defensive cultures cannot easily adapt in the long term. They could be successful in the short-run, and some are highly successful at some point in their histories. However, they were unable to continue success when markets turned because they could not respond quickly enough to changing business conditions. Key characteristics of defensive cultures are that they:

- Focus on short-term results

- Emphasize structure and systems

- Value one group (customers, stockholders, or employees) at the expense of others

- Maintain biased perceptions of the competition (if competition *is* considered!)

- Engender discomfort over expressing negative thoughts

- Hold illusions of invulnerability

- Ignore alternative strategies

The hard truth—changing culture is not easy to do. True culture change may take years—and the larger the organization or the more entrenched the current culture, the longer change may take. Leaders who are successful on this journey commit to be in it for the long haul.

NINE STEPS

The following is a list of nine steps I recommend for leading culture change:

- **Take off the "rose colored" glasses.** You need to be open to what you might find about your organization when you look beyond "espoused values."

- **Observe patterns of behavior.** How do people behave to "fit in" with your organization? Which of these patterns are helpful? Which ones limit high performance as a company? (Hint: Ask people to describe what is expected for them to succeed in your organization.)

- **Identify underlying assumptions and beliefs.** Remember culture is framed by what we assume to be true about our organization and our environment. Talk to people to identify assumptions that seem to drive behaviors you observe.

- **Determine which assumptions are no longer helpful.** Are some assumptions about your company or your environment no longer true in today's world? Do some assumptions limit your organization's ability to meet new or changing demands?

- **Determine how those assumptions are reinforced right now.** You can refer to the body of this article for hints about what to look for.

- **State the new assumption.** It is important to provide a *new* framework for people to 1) help them interpret the demands of their environment and 2) inform their reactions.

- **Pick one or two key leverage points** where you can start making concrete changes to neutralize old assumptions and reinforce new beliefs.

- **Use your power, position, influence, and/or authority to make those changes a reality.**

- **As those changes start to become embedded, look for more leverage points** to systematically reinforce the new assumptions, until they are just "part of the culture."

MAKING TIME TO THINK

When was the last time you had a really good "think?" You know, the kind that was reflective, productive, and creative? The kind that produced new ideas, perceptions, or awareness? The kind of thinking that helps you tap into your own wisdom to solve problems more productively?   If this kind of thinking and think time seems like a luxury to you these days, you are not alone!

The pressure to "produce" at work has never been higher. With global competition and technological advances, we are faced with the need to be more and more productive, with greater and greater urgency. Unfortunately, this most often translates into holding more meetings and plowing through more mail, with less time for actual *thinking*.

The reality is that strategy, innovation, and breakthroughs *depend* on our ability to think well, which means taking the time and having the discipline to do it. Unfortunately, scurrying around from place to place or being glued to your screen provides little time to reflect on information, see patterns, identify new approaches, consider options, or weigh consequences. As a result, external pressure may force reactive and suboptimal decisions.

Quality think time is distraction free. Here are some tips to regain it.

- Turn off your email for 30 minutes.

- Turn off your smart phone for 30 minutes.

- If your desk is too distracting, go to an unused conference or work room for 30 minutes.

- Create a standing appointment on your own calendar for focused think/work time.

- Tell your secretary/kids/colleagues not to bother you for 30 minutes unless there is a life-threatening emergency. Discuss the definition of "life threatening."

- Keep a private journal (electronic or otherwise) to record your reflections, ideas, and insights. You don't want to lose them now that you have them!

If you are having difficulty focusing, even when you have carved out some think time for yourself, here are some things that help me:

- Breathe deeply to calm your mind.

- Make a list of everything you need to think about and attend to. Then pick one.

- Set a timer and commit to focus on this one topic for 20-30 minutes.

- When time is up, permit yourself to stop, take a break, or if you are really on a roll, extend your think time for another 20-30 minutes.

- Consider adding physical activity (such as a walk) to quell any "antsy-ness" and take your thinking to the next level.

I recognize people have different styles and preferences in *how* they think—and whatever works for you is great. But I do suggest you honor that process within yourself and make it a priority to give yourself the time and space to do it. Who knows, you might just change your world!

Cathy Perme

Part 2:
Getting Along

Confucius understood change did not happen without the people's consent. He also knew having influence meant more than being powerful—it meant embracing and empowering people to be their best. That was the essence of humanity to him.

> *If you want to make a stand, help others make a stand, and if you want to reach your goal, help others reach their goal. Consider yourself and treat others accordingly; this is the method of humanity.* (6.29)

> *The noble-minded encourage what is beautiful in people and discourage what is ugly in them. Little people do the opposite.* (12.16)

And he had a prescription for developing effective teamwork, because humanity and integrity were so important to him:

Don't grieve when people fail to recognize your ability. Grieve when you fail to recognize theirs. (1.16)

Above all else, be loyal and stand by your words... And when you're wrong, don't be afraid to change. (1.8)

The following essays arise from the struggle of being an effective team player—both as a participant and a leader—and learning how to trust oneself and others in the process.

TEAMS—CAN WE, OR CAN'T WE?[4]

Can we get along in a team setting or not? Can we give the other person (you know which one—the one we "never could stand," the one that "just doesn't fit in") the credit for an idea that could very possibly make things better? Can we admit someone else has the answer we've been seeking?

These are just a few of the questions individuals face when confronted with working in a team. Most people are comfortable with the concept: "two heads are better than one." When this concept is put into practice however, one should not expect immediate results. A group of individuals cannot be expected to operate as a team just because they call themselves a team. Further, teamwork is even harder to create in long-existing work groups.

Every individual who boards a work team carries baggage that can extend from an overnight bag to a steamer-sized trunk fully equipped for a two-week cruise. While checking in the baggage, we find a large suitcase full of "can't stand 'ems" and a trunk filled with "doesn't fit ins." A closer inspection of a satchel reveals an incident back in October of 2005 when someone's authority was undermined. That large blue bag contains the time three years ago when someone was passed over for a promotion, and the small valise holds an occasion last week when someone was publicly chastised for an error he/she did not commit.

We need to be aware of the impact baggage has on relationships. Those bags of perceptions stem from real "hurts" people have experienced in the past. People won't drop these bags until they can resolve that hurt, or trust they won't be hurt (intentionally) the same way again.

Sometimes we need to slow down to go fast. Most people want to get into tasks quickly and can't understand why their efforts seem so labored. By slowing down to air feelings, to share hopes and fears, and to resolve long-standing conflicts, we just might be able to work a lot faster.

DO'S AND DON'TS FOR
BUILDING TEAM RELATIONSHIPS

DO:

- Realize your perception is *your* reality—not everyone else's.

- Risk honesty and openness.

- Be sensitive to people's feelings.

- Speak from your own experience.

- Check out your perceptions.

- Be patient.

- Realize this is something new and there is no "tried-and-true" formula to follow.

- Be willing to give up some control.

- Take responsibility for your part in a difficult relationship.

- Admit you do not have all the answers, or even know all the questions.

- Believe everyone has something to offer.

- Ask plainly for what you want from another person.

- Listen.

- Be willing to compromise.

DON'T:

- Assume everyone thinks like you.

- Expect everyone to participate equally.

- Demand that others change first.

- Expect that all your expectations will be met.

- "Should" on each other—that's a form of blaming and shaming.

- Give up at the first sign of tension or conflict.

Most people have been holding on to their bags for a long time, and it will take more time before they loosen their grip. Patience, sensitivity, and consistent behavior will help people trust that everybody (including themselves) wins when they let go.

Building Trust

Did you know "trust," "true," and "tree" all have the same root? The word was brought into Old English from a Nordic word meaning "hard wood." So "trust" was meant to be strong, durable, and real. Like a tree, it may take a long time to grow and can easily be cut down. Webster's definition of trust is "assured reliance on the character, ability, strength, or truth of someone or something" (Merriam-Webster, 2017).

Character: When we trust someone's character, we trust they will act responsibly and beyond their own interests. We trust they care about us and will consider us when making decisions that affect us.

Ability: When we trust someone's ability, we trust they are skilled and competent to successfully accomplish the task at hand.

Strength: When we trust someone's strength, we trust they will make commitments, follow through, and have the courage to support us.

Truth: When we trust someone's truth, we trust the information they provide is complete and accurate, and that they clearly represent their own feelings, motivations, and interpretations.

What Does It Mean to Trust Yourself?

Trusting yourself means becoming aware of your own values and motivations, and being honest with yourself about your feelings and conflicts. This helps sort out the multitude of issues that bombard us every day. We can then recognize those issues we need to act on and those we do not.

Trusting yourself also means relying on your senses, your intelligence, your experience, and your knowledge to provide the information you need to make the right decisions.

What Does It Mean to Trust Others?

When we first start working with someone, we do not really have enough information to trust them. Trust builds as we experience the relationship.

At first, trusting others means going beyond our personal fears, communicating what we want, and asking for clarification if something is different from what we expected.

As we gain experience, trusting others means acknowledging what we do trust about them and what we do not. For example, I might trust the character, strength and truth of an associate but not his or her ability in a particular area. Or I might trust that person's character and ability but not their follow-through. In communicating what we do and do not trust, we have an opportunity to work together to repair trust, to build on each other's strengths, and to grow the relationship.

How to Build It

- **Make commitments.** If you are always on the fence, people will not know how to rely on you.

- **Follow through on commitments.** Have you promised to send an article to someone? Do it. If you follow through on minor commitments, people will trust you to follow through on major commitments.

- **Be on time for appointments, and return phone calls, messages, and emails on a timely basis.** The time we give to others is a major commitment. If you honor that, people will trust the reliability of your other commitments.

- **Be honest about your motivations.** People can smell a hidden agenda, miles away.

- **Be honest about your skills and knowledge.** You want people to trust your competency, and part of that is admitting what you do not know and then getting help.

- **Be clear about your expectations.** You increase the trust level by being truthful about what you want or expect, and what your boundaries are.

- **Check out inconsistent messages.** Sometimes we misinterpret other's behavior because their personality or culture is different from ours.

- **Rely on others to help you.** Success depends on trusting other people to help you. Blending the best talents and abilities on a team ends with success for everyone.

Empowering Others[5]

Many people have no idea how to empower others, and one can't learn simply through a textbook or course. Empowering others means "letting go." It means making a systematic and sustained effort to give others more information, knowledge, support, and opportunities to exercise their power for mutual benefit.

An empowering leader has the courage to ask more questions than give answers and effectively focuses the team on shared vision, values, and goals. In this role the leader collects, transforms, and disseminates information, creating dialog within the team.

What Does An Empowering Leader Do?

1. **Asks productive questions**. This is critical. Productive questions stimulate the team to im-

prove their own thinking and problem-solving processes. They are thoughtful and probing in nature. They do not focus on facts and figures, but on concepts, feelings, values, and strategies.

2. **Maintains balance**. The leader is like the pilot of a sailboat—listening, looking, and testing the environment to identify risks and opportunities. She/he transforms that information for the team, helping to set realistic expectations for performance. By doing so, the leader helps the team stay balanced and use the forces of change to move toward the goal.

3. **Manages boundaries**. Too much information can distract and distress; too little can result in inaction. The leader identifies information and other resources the team needs and ensures boundaries are removed to make them available. The leader also recognizes information that is irrelevant and establishes boundaries to slow down or redirect that information to parts of the organization where it may be needed.

4. **Focuses attention on vision, values, and goals**. Through choice of questions, clearly state expectation, and effective boundaries management, an empowering leader infuses

vision, values, and goals into the daily work of the team.

An empowering leader is at the center, not the head, of an effective team. He or she is neither greater nor less than any other member of the group— but simply contributes different things to the team's overall success.

How Do Empowering Leaders Behave?

A disempowering person says:

- Your problem is...

- Why are you doing that? Here's what you should do.

- I'm not paying you to think.

- Here's the plan. Follow it. I want a full report in 6 months.

- I hope you learned something from this.

- Believe me, if you need to know something I'll tell you.

- Forget what you are doing, this is more important.

- You should be happy because…

- I hope you're satisfied.

An empowering leader says:

- What issues are you struggling with on this?

- What does the client want?

- What is your strategy for...

- How does that fit our vision, values, and goals?

- In evaluating your work/project, what are you proud of? Sorry about? What have you learned?

- This is what's important to me...

- What information do you need?

- Who else should be involved, and when?

- How can I help you succeed?

TERRORIZED!
DEALING WITH GROUP BULLIES

I have seen more than a few groups struggle with what I would call group "bullies." You know these folks—the ones who talk the loudest and most often, seem to take control, and pretty much get what they want. They may intimidate us by their sheer forcefulness, and often succeed by injecting havoc into a group. The rest of us feel as stunned, as if a tidal wave had hit us. Not knowing how to react, we may respond weakly or badly, feeling foolish as the bully continues to dominate.

Now, I can't write this without admitting I've been accused of having been a group "bully" myself at times. I earned this title when I was passionate about something I thought was important, but no one else seemed to take any interest! But did I set out to be a bully? No.

Here are the top reasons I have found people either bully or feel bullied by someone in a group:

- **The purpose is not clear**. If the reason the group or team exists is murky, it creates the opportunity to impose a personal agenda, which is often the motive behind bully behavior.

- **Meeting objectives and desired outcomes are foggy**. If there are no clear objectives for a meeting (i.e. decide "x," brainstorm about "y," etc.) a potential bully may see this as an invitation to take control.

- **Decision-making is unclear**. This is often the case when there are other leaders or committees involved, and it is not clear who is making what decision with whose input. Someone may attempt to dominate to fill an apparent void.

- **The rules of engagement are not spelled out**. Are group members expected to represent and advocate for others or do they represent themselves? What is the expected level of participation? How are members expected to communicate their concerns and ideas? What are the "ground rules"? If there are no stated protocols, the confusion can usher in dominating behavior.

- **There are no consequences for adverse behavior.** Sadly, there are often "covert consequences" that have a negative impact on the people involved—such as ostracism, backbiting, or a group that slowly falls apart. The group needs to define and agree to consequences *up front* to allow interventions with unacceptable behavior on a timely basis. Otherwise, you are left hoping a facilitator or leader will notice the problem and do something.

I have found once these are clearly identified, bullying behavior virtually disappears. Keep in mind people rarely set out to become "bullies" and most often just want to be heard! By setting a clear focus, decision-making norms, and rules of engagement, groups can ensure everyone can contribute to achieving the goals of the group, respectfully and effectively.

A Facilitator's Intervention Approach

Here is a five-step approach[6] I have used in dealing with problem behavior in a group.
.

- **Level 1: Do nothing.** That's right, do nothing. See if this person will catch him/herself or notice the body language of others and realize his/her actions are not helpful.

- **Level 2: Refer to ground rules.** If the behavior persists, remind the group in general about the ground rules, paying particular attention to the one being challenged. If there is no ground rule, suggest setting one.

- **Level 3: Redirect.** If the behavior persists, actively intervene to move the discussion along. You may need to interrupt the speaker and redirect the conversation, or suggest a different process that avoids the opportunity for this behavior.

- **Level 4: Off-line Feedback.** If the behavior persists, you can probably assume the person is either clueless about their impact, frustrated with the group, or both. Help that person find a different way to express him or herself, or to accept the direction of the group.

- **Level 5: In-group Feedback:** If the behavior continues, stop the process and ask the other group members to give that person feedback about their reaction to this person's behavior and message. This can be uncomfortable and needs to be done respectfully. But my experience is you'll only have to do this once!

THE BEST TEAM TRAINING EVER!

Have you ever seen improvisational comedy or instant theater at places like comedy clubs or dinner theaters? It's a marvel to watch. Given just a few suggestions from the audience, an empty stage, and no time to think, the cast always seems to pull off an inventive and fun skit. How do they do it?

One year, I decided to take some lessons in "improv" to learn how to be less intense. (Those of you who know me may laugh now!) I attended Brave New Workshop's (Minnesota) Improvisation Classes for 9 months. I found that to succeed in improvisation, one does not need to be a quick wit or have a steady stream of jokes, thankfully. One simply needs to be a good team player. What guides team play are eight basic rules (Kliesen Wehrman, 1994).

8 Basic Rules of Improvisation[7]

1. Concentrate—You and your partners are making a whole new reality. Nobody is boss, so nobody knows what's next. The scene is made in the space between you. Pay attention, or you'll miss it.

2. Trust—You've got everything you need. So does your partner.

3. Give and take—Take turns!

4. Make assumptions—Observe out loud what you are discovering.

5. Say "Yes, and..."/ Do not negate—First acknowledge the truth in what was just said and add a piece of observation to it.

6. Work at the top of your intelligence—Don't play at the locker-room level. Any 7th-grader can do that.

7. Choose the action—Physically doing what you are thinking conveys millions of unspoken observations. It leads you to *discover* rather than *invent.*

8. Remember you can have anything you want in the scene—You can be anybody. You can use any object. You can be anywhere. Cool.

As I learned to play with a team of actors, I realized these rules apply to every team I am on, from product development to training, from business to family. Here's what I learned:

- **Trust**—I never realized how little I trusted myself or others in any given situation! When I started to affirm I have everything I need (my 5 senses, my intelligence, my experiences, my feelings, my observations) to succeed, and my partners did too, I found myself controlling less and enjoying more in the process.

- **Give & Take**—I never realized that this depended so deeply on trust. (If I don't trust you or myself, I'm going to set up the scene or process to ensure I get what I want.)

- **"Yes, and..."**—In improvisation, "yes, but..." kills a skit in no time flat. If actors negate each other's ideas rather than build on them, the scene never gets off the ground. So too in work teams, where time is no less precious.

- **Clarify Assumptions**—All of us constantly operate from assumptions we have made about people, places, or situations. Stating those assumptions clearly helps avoid miscommunication down the line.

Remember, we can remake ourselves every day, in every situation. Try just one of these techniques at your next team meeting. You may be surprised at the results, and even find yourself saying "Cool!"

PART 3:
MANAGING CHANGE (YOURS!)

Confucius lived to the ripe old age of 78, which was a very long time in 2500 BC! He spoke eloquently about his own change and growth over time:

> *At fifteen I devoted myself to learning, and at thirty stood firm. At forty I had no doubts, and at fifty understood the Mandate of Heaven. At sixty I listened with effortless accord. And at seventy I followed the mind's passing fancies without overstepping any bounds.* (2.4)

To Confucius, learning was key to success and the means to nobility. Learning from mistakes, reflecting thoughtfully, and acting on what you learned were vitally important.

To learn and never think—that's delusion. But to think and never learn—that is perilous indeed! (2.15)

Worthy admonitions cannot fail to inspire us, but what matters is changing ourselves. Reverent advice cannot fail to encourage us, but what matters is acting upon it. Encouraged without acting, inspired without changing—there's nothing to be done for such people. (9.24)

He also had a pretty good sense of humor and outlook about getting feedback about himself and his own mistakes:

How lucky I am. If I make a mistake, someone is sure to recognize it. (7.31)

A person's various faults are all of a piece. Recognizing your faults is a way of understanding Humanity. (4.7)

As a result, I make the case the only person you can change is yourself, and taking a leadership role demands that you manage yourself well in the face of change, or you will not be able to lead effectively. The following essays look at managing your own change, from situations that go from changing small habits to dealing with major life issues.

Getting Trapped in Your Success

Like me, you've no doubt had successes in your life, achievements that make you proud—areas where you did your best, and your effort was rewarded. It feels great, doesn't it? The question is; how do we sustain that feeling?

What traps most of us is relying more and more on what made us successful, without thinking about what success means. So, we rely on knowledge, skills, or old formulas that may become increasingly overextended and out of touch. We stop learning. We become tired and tiring. It's like the old adage: "When all you've got is a hammer, everything looks like a nail." Our strengths become our weaknesses, and what caused our success now causes our failure.

Organizations, as well as people, can be trapped in their own success. When organizations believe they have nothing more to learn, they begin to suffer what the Greeks called "hubris," loosely translated as "arrogance." In almost every Greek tragedy, the heroes overcame tremendous odds to succeed but failed in the end because their own ego blinded them to what was important.

It is important to view the need for change as a measure of success, not failure. Change, learning, and growth are the only things that will ensure continued success. When we get to the point where we have almost mastered something, it's time to start learning something new.

True danger lies in the zone between mastery and the next learning cycle. Maybe we disengage and go into autopilot, or maybe we create crises for ourselves and others just to relieve boredom. Maybe we distract ourselves with meaningless activities. In any case, the decline starts here.

How do we as individuals and organizations stop this self-defeating cycle?

First, we need to watch for anomalies—signs of boredom, little cracks in the facade, things that don't fit into our current worldview.

Second, we need to continually set aside time to reflect on where we've been, where we're going, and how we feel about it. Reflection is an under-utilized, incredibly powerful tool. Most vacations, planning sessions, or training workshops are so busy we really don't have time to reflect.

Third, we need to have the discipline to leap to a new learning cycle even when things are going well.

Fourth, we need to have the courage to learn deeply, to go to places within ourselves where we may feel totally confused and out-of-sorts, before emerging with new understandings and insights.

Are You Trapped?[8] (O'Neill, 1993)

- Do you find yourself in a frantic whirl of commitments?

- Do you compete out of habit?

- Is winning central to your identity?

- Have the symbols of success or status become crucial to your self-worth?

- Do you abuse or rely too much on your natural talents?

- Have you found yourself blaming problems on other people or external factors?

- Do you brood on bad news or criticism?

- Do you have almost a compulsive need to control?

- Do you find yourself getting angry over little things, or do you occasionally surprise yourself with intense emotions that seem out of proportion to the situation?

- Are you becoming rigid in your views, finding it hard to listen to other points of view?

If you answered yes to any of the above questions, spend some time reflecting on what success means to you. If you don't find yourself in this list, look again. You may be denying some inner secrets that could hurt you if left untended.

WHEN OLD HABITS DIE HARD

When I bought my first iPad I was irked to find only a half-sheet of paper with any instructions about how to use it. Where is the manual, I thought? Even after getting it up and running, I continued to find myself short of patience about how to make it work at times. I wanted my manual! This was (and still is) my dilemma in working with the explosion of new technologies available today, which are supposed to be completely intuitive. I've been so well programmed to cater to the intricacies and whims of computers in the past, I have no idea how to be intuitive with them now, and I can barely keep up with what they all can do.

Which brings me to wonder, in what other parts of my life do old habits die hard? As a change agent, I pride myself on being able to spot trends, embrace change, and help others steer through theirs. However, I notice the more experience I have, the more "set in my ways" I become. I'd like to think it means there are just more neurons that need to be "synced up" with new ideas in my brain. At the same time, I have an uneasy feeling I just might be (shall I dare say it?) resistant to change.

My colleague, Ian Sutherland, a change manager in the UK, describes two kinds of resistance to change—active resistance and inertia. Sometimes resistance to change *is* active, in which a person really objects to what is being proposed. More often it is inertia, which is resistance to changing the status quo. Let's face it, it is just easier to stay the way we are.

The problem with inertia, both in organizations and ourselves, is the world can pass us by before we even notice it. To stay nimble and sharp, we need to grow continually. That means challenging old habits now and then to see if they still apply.

At the same time, it is important to balance the need for change and growth with what is critical and sacrosanct. Old habits *became* habits for good reason; that may still hold true. We need to be critical and guard those that still add value and support. These anchors will help us embrace the other aspects of a given change.

So how can we both embrace change and honor what we already know? Personally and organizationally, it is about being willing to experiment. Being proactive about trying something new, reflecting on your experience with it, and making clear decisions to keep or discard it gives you more power to steer your own course in a changing world.

It is also important to be prepared to invest in the experiment. To make anything new work will obviously require effort and time, but may also need some financial investment for training, equipment, or support. In a wider sense, investment may also mean helping others who may be challenged by the changes we make.

TRY A PERSONAL EXPERIMENT!

1. **Decide on something new to try**. Pick one idea or opportunity at a time. Set some personal criteria in advance to help you decide if the change is positive.

2. **Really give it a shot.** Set a trial period and give it your all. Notice any patterns or results you are seeing but withhold judgment until your trial period is up.

3. **Accept help.** You can't be a pro at everything, so be willing to learn from someone who can teach you.

4. **Reflect on your experience.** After you've worked with this new change for a while, con-

sider its impact on you, your work or life style, and your customers. Did it deliver what you hoped? Were there any surprises? Do the advantages outweigh the costs?

5. **ONLY THEN, decide if this is for you.** Now is the time to be selective, to decide what you will keep or discard.

This world will keep changing more rapidly than ever, so to stand still is not a sustainable option. The beginning of a new job or a new year is a great time to try something new. Why not challenge an old habit of yours?

Dealing with a Changing Culture

In our daily work lives, we orient ourselves with something known as organizational culture. ***Organizational culture is an invisible web of values and expectations that bonds the group together.*** When there is rapid cultural change in our organization, we may lose our point of reference and feel a sense of upheaval. Some may even feel a profound sense of loss. Although organizational cultures share many similarities, each is unique with its own rules and touchstones.

At IBM, for instance, where I spent 12 rewarding years early in my career, the prevailing touchstone was a sense of "family." Like other families, membership in the IBM family was unconditional. A lifetime guaranteed job was part of that unconditional acceptance. Over time, as the company responded to a new and different market place, the culture underwent a significant change—a team concept replaced "family," where acceptance was conditional, based on contribution. Lifetime job security was out. Employees were expected to be entrepreneurial and add value to the bottom line.

Even though I clearly understood the need for change, as a former employee, I was saddened to see the old IBM go—I had great memories of it and the warm cocoon it generated. I know how hard it was for some of my former colleagues to deal with it.

I also believe change brings tremendous opportunity to create something new, if people can learn to adapt to it. Here are some ways I found that work:

- **Accept change is a process that never ends.** Even cultures that seem to be stable are always undergoing constant change. One way to embrace change is to get involved in shaping it.

- **Allow yourself to grieve the past.** Find the parts of the past you value, and create a transition ritual to help you let go. Share your concerns, grief, and questions with those you trust.

- **Remember you have choices.** Culture change is neither good nor bad. When you are in the midst of it, you need to search your own soul and ask: "Do I accept the change? Do I want to be a part of it?"

- **Take care of yourself.** Eat right and get plenty of rest and exercise. Create a personal vision to help guide you through turbulent times.

TIPS FOR DEALING WITH A CHANGING CULTURE

DO:

- Acknowledge that something is changing.

- Expect ambivalence.

- Expect upheaval.

- Recognize the strengths of the past.

- Create a transition ritual to help you let go.

- Get organized to be effective.

- Recognize your feelings and understand you may have conflicting emotions.

- Be open with allies and confidantes.

- Embrace change.

DON'T:

- Try to hang on to the past.

- Bury your feelings.

- Forget the big picture.

- Overlook opportunities that change might bring.

- Forget what's important to you

- Neglect to make your own plans.

- Carry hidden agendas.

- Be afraid to ask for help.

- Be inflexible.

CREATING YOUR FUTURE

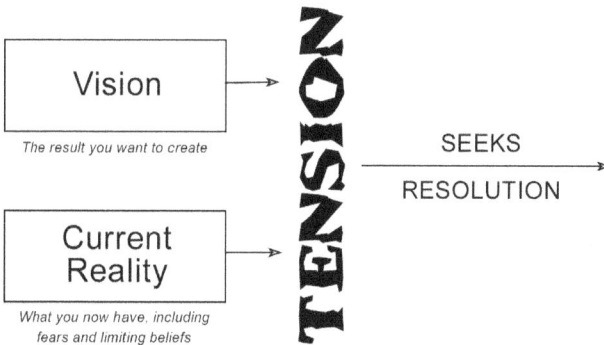

Have you ever noticed when you have something clearly in mind you can't rest until it's a reality? Say you really wanted a bright red sports car—what would happen when you pulled out onto the highway every day?

That experience is called "creative tension"[9] and is what artists feel when they stare at a blank canvas or an uncut piece of stone and can see exactly what they want to create. ***Creative or structural tension is the gap between what you want (vision) and what you have (current reality) (Fritz, 1984; Senge, 2006). It can be a powerful force*** you can tap to create what you want in your life.

The key behind this is *holding* the tension until your reality matches your vision. That is more easily said than done. Tension is uncomfortable and usually thought of as something to eliminate. The gap between a vision and reality can seem overwhelming—so we compromise our vision ("We've set our sights too high!") or deny our reality ("It's really not so bad after all!") to eliminate that gnawing feeling the gap produces. As a result, dreams and visions can become watered down over time, and it's easy to settle back into mediocrity.

Cultivating creative tension means thinking like an artist. It means holding your vision firmly in mind and acknowledging and embracing current reality at the same time. It means making choices, taking action, and living with ambiguity.

HOW CAN YOU CREATE EFFECTIVELY?

1. **Determine what you want.** Be clear about what you want and describe it to yourself and others in as much detail as possible.

2. **Acknowledge reality.** Be objective and assess your reality much like a reporter would. Watch your denial systems! Ask others what they see, to help you see different perspectives.

3. *Choose* **what you want.** This is a powerful step. There is a difference between want and will—making an active choice puts your personal power behind it.

4. **Determine what you must do, _today,_ to make this a reality.** The act of creating something is not a one-time event. Seeing this as a process will help you become more of an artist.

5. **Do it.** Take action!

6. **Let go of the results.** This may seem paradoxical, but if you worry or try to control outcomes you will only corrupt the creative process. Realize reality changes, and tomorrow you have another chance to act.

Cathy Perme

Adjusting Your Sails

*"We may not be able to control the direction
of the wind, but we can adjust our sails."*
James Dean, American Actor

Colin Duggleby was one of the best leaders I ever met. As CEO of a mid-sized company in the UK, he had a depth of wisdom and compassion I have found rare when working with top executives. He was 50 years old and on top of the world—leading a company, staying fit by running, and recently married to the love of his life.

When doctors diagnosed his persistent stomach pain not as an ulcer, but as a very aggressive, incurable form of cancer, he was shocked to hear he had only four to nine months to live. Can you imagine it? He was at the top of his game, and the game was being called.

Colin was mad. I heard from colleagues he was having a difficult time accepting his fate; it was hard for them to comfort him. When I talked to him on the phone one day, he voiced terrible frustration about his "death sentence."

I had a plaque hanging in my office that had a lot of meaning for me. It was a quote by James Dean, the American actor: "You can't control the direction of the wind, but you can adjust your sails." On a whim, I wrapped it up and sent it to Colin with a note. That was the last contact I had with him.

A few months after his death, I got a thank-you letter from his widow, Valerie. She said the gift and the message on the plaque were significant to Colin, and helped him to focus on making the most of the time he *did* have. That plaque now hangs in the hospice where he died, for others to see and appreciate.

In many ways, large or small, we may not get what we want or deserve. A slow economy, continuing job losses, ongoing mergers and acquisitions, health problems—all are prevailing winds over which we may have little control. Compounded by family or relationship concerns, these may seem overwhelming.

Tips for "Adjusting Your Sails"

People don't resist change, they resist loss. In adapting to change, we succeed to the extent we can face loss and make new choices.

1. It is not only OK, but it is *important*, to mourn the loss. Even if the loss is simply a habit that is no longer good for us or is something significant like a job loss, divorce or death, we need to be able to mourn it. We have to be able to gripe and grouse, rage and rail, or collapse in a depressed puddle because that is what will allow us to move on.

2. Find someone with whom you can share your sadness, hopes, and fears, as well as bounce ideas and get feedback. This can be a friend or a paid professional, but you want someone who will provide encouragement as well as a good butt-kicking when you need it.

3. Get medical help if you need it. Meds can do wonderful things to help a person function through a painful loss. Strong people recognize when they need help.

4. Make the choice to be happy. Studies have shown people who *choose* to be happy actually *are* happier. Why? Because that one

fundamental choice creates a cascade of other choices in terms of attitudes, skills, jobs, relationships, and life styles.

5. With new eyes, do an inventory of yourself—what is important to you, what you are good at, and what others value about you? Then think about where and how you can find that "sweet spot" where these three intersect.

6. And lastly, give it time. Don't expect instant results. You can still reach your destination—but perhaps in a different way, with new eyes, new experiences, and a new appreciation of the fine specimen of humanity you are!

Colin's story reminds us, even in the direst of circumstances, we can make choices. We can: (1) choose to act like victims, (2) choose to fight back, or (3) choose to steer our ship differently. Colin's legacy continued in the company he led, with the annual Colin Duggleby Award, given to an employee who best exemplified Colin's ability to appreciate people and care deeply about mission and values. May he rest in peace. He is fondly remembered.

PART 4: FINDING BALANCE

This is one area in which Confucius doesn't have much to say, probably with good reason. His work seemed to be all-encompassing, with the exception that he loved poetry. He lived at a time in which women had strict roles for maintaining the home and child-rearing, and men did not have to deal with these "distractions" from their focus. About the only thing Confucius said about balance in life is this:

Dwell at home in humility. Conduct your business in reverence. And in your dealings with others, be faithful. (13.19)

Today we all have more options in life and need to balance "day-to-day living" with "making a living," which can be hard to do, especially if you are passionate about your work. For instance, I've been a workaholic, and I don't like it. I find much more joy in a balanced life, but that has taken a long time coming. Thus, the essays that follow are about seeking a balanced life and recognizing, perhaps, it is ever-evolving.

So, what are we left with? No matter where we end up in our lives, Confucius said it best:

> *To learn, and then, in its due season, put what you have learned into practice—isn't that still a great pleasure? And to have a friend visit from somewhere far away—isn't that still a great joy? When you're ignored by the world like this, and yet bear no resentment—isn't that great nobility?* (1.1)

> *My life has been my prayer.* (7.35)

When Life Intrudes

I once heard a high-powered speaker talk about how to get neatly and tightly focused in life and business—like a lean, mean, strategic machine. As I scribbled notes full of good advice and intention, I had a recurring thought: I must be living in a parallel universe!

My universe is one in which business meetings can be interrupted by the needs of a sick child, focus can be distracted by family concerns, and fatigue or stress can drain energy from the day. I don't think I am alone.

There is an old saying: "life is what happens when you are planning something else." Sometimes life intrudes in shocking or unpredictable ways—such as when a loved one dies, someone loses a job, or becomes seriously ill. Most often life intrudes in little ways on a daily basis—a child wants your attention, your mate is mad at you, the school needs paperwork, etc.

When life intrudes, it distracts our attention and saps our energy. It is hard to focus on anything for very long. And for competitive spirits like me, it can make us feel dissatisfied with what we are able to achieve.

What I realized is *life is not an intrusion*—it *is* life! And as M. Scott Peck (1978) wrote in *The Road Less Traveled*, life is difficult, and it is messy. It squirts out sideways and gums up the lean, mean, strategic machine. And in the end, life is what counts.

So, for other competitive spirits like me, here are a few things I have learned over the years—while being a business owner, management consultant, wife, mother, daughter, sister, friend, author, and community volunteer— about what it means to balance work and life in the parallel universe.

- No, it isn't fair.

- It is critical to recognize your own limits—otherwise you could begin a downward spiral by continually committing too much.

- Acceptance helps you focus—by accepting the whole of your life, you can make better decisions about where and how to focus your energy, which is one of your most precious commodities.

- Self-care is important—it helps maintain energy and perspective. Taking time to do this is not a sacrifice of time; it is an investment in energy.

- You can do anything you want in life—just one thing at a time.

Cathy Perme

SEEKING THE BALANCED LIFE[10]

For the last twenty years, I have sought the balanced life. I came to the conclusion there is no such thing as a balanced life. There may be only a balanced *approach* to life.

The difference lies in our image of balance, and how it applies to our work and lives. I learned "balance" really has two meanings. The first implies a sense of stability; the second, a sense of movement.

Think of a top, which can turn faster and faster as long as its weight is evenly distributed. This is the model of balance many of us grew up with and have internalized. This model implies if we just go fast enough, we can do it all and have it all. Balancing ourselves means being good at calendar management and to-do lists, so we do not waste a moment of time. The belief is we can lead a balanced life if we just divvy it up and manage it correctly. The dangers are becoming "top heavy" by focusing too much in one area, or being "off-balance" by inadequate time management.

The second image of balance describes movement. Think of a dancer who "moves forward and back ... wavers slightly; tilts and returns to equilibrium." (Webster's New World College Dictionary 4th Edition, 1999, p. 108) This is a more dynamic definition of balance, suggesting we are constantly stepping out, regrouping, and starting again. If we approach work and life like a dancer, we are always in the midst of falling. Every step we take trusts our ability to keep from doing so.

Somehow, this image of balance as "dance" is more freeing to me. There is a recognition that being off-balance is a normal part of life and a necessary condition of forward movement. It also means I need to trust myself when it comes to choosing where to focus my time and energy, rather than trying to stabilize a lot of competing interests.

Balance as "dance" is a more challenging metaphor too. It means we must make choices and accept our limitations. As a wise woman once said to me, "You can do everything you want in life, just one thing at a time."

Learning to Balance in the Dance of Life

Speed: One can choose to waltz versus mambo. That means monitoring one's energy level and deciding how fast to dance.

There is nothing wrong with cutting back on work hours or commitments until one has the energy for them. In fact, it is the sane thing to do.

Focus: In traditional ballrooms, dances are played in sets. One signs up to dance a set of three similar dances with the same partner, or can choose to sit out a set. By focusing this way, the dancer deepens the experience and has an opportunity to improve skill with each dance in the set.

At work or at home, this means choosing one or two areas to focus on and do well. Or it may mean taking a needed break to regroup before the next major push.

Complexity: There are many levels of difficulty in dance, and it takes energy and patience to learn new moves. It is when one is learning that one is most off-balance.

At work or at home, this means giving oneself time and permission to "wobble" while learn-

ing and experiencing new things. It also means taking a break now and then to regain confidence by doing something one does well!

COPING WITH
SUPER-CHARGED CHANGE

There are times in our lives when change seems "super-charged," when it shakes the very foundation of who we are. Emotions run deep, what we fear may very well be reality, and we may be powerless to control or influence the change itself.

I experienced such change over a period of six months many years ago, and the memories of that time are still powerful for me. It was the time while my husband and I waited and waited to adopt our daughter. Five times we had travel dates. Four times we were canceled, sometimes at the last minute. Each time I felt like a toy boat on a beach, hit by a tidal wave that would not stop. I feared we would not get our daughter. I feared for my business. I feared for my soul because I was running out of hope.

In my head, I knew about "change" and what I should expect. In my heart, I was shocked at the pain and felt it would never end. I felt like I was "losing it." This is what I learned about coping when you cannot influence the change itself:

- **Information**—This was critical to me because I was desperate to understand the situation. Even negative information was better than none. When I had no information, I made up my own stories about what was happening, which made me feel more powerless. To help myself, I read a lot, I found a reliable information source, and I checked out rumors.

- **Reliable contacts**—Talking to others who survived the process was helpful, although timing was important. In the initial shock stage, I did not want to talk to others who had succeeded. I just wanted to wallow for a while with someone who could sympathize. When I was ready to emerge, I looked to the stories of those who were successful to provide hope.

- **Choices**—This was the most important to me—recognizing my choice(s). When I realized I could stop participating in this particular adoption program, I felt more empowered. I started to see and evaluate my options. Although I chose to remain, it was an *active* decision to live with the uncertainty of the process, and as a result, I felt less like a victim.

TIPS FOR GETTING THROUGH IT

1. Find one person you can trust to give you objective information without sensation. Ask that person to be honest about the bad news as well as the good. Arrange to get regular updates; initiate them yourself, if necessary.

2. Don't rely on the "network" (whether it is a people network or an electronic network) to provide you with accurate information about what is happening. What you will get are rumors or information without context. Make sure you check things out with your contact person before taking any news to heart.

3. Find at least one or two other people you can trust. Talk to them about the change and its impact on you. If you don't want suggestions, ask that they just listen for now. If you don't have someone in your circle that you can trust, consider outside resources like a therapist or support group.

4. Take an inventory of your current and/or potential losses. Then decide if there is something you can do to minimize or make up for

each loss.

5. Make a decision—a choice. Even though you can't change what happened, you can decide your personal approach.

"Super-charged" change is showing up more often in our work lives with continued restructurings, layoffs, and new technologies that impact our perceptions of who we are and what we do, and in our personal lives with illnesses and traumatic events. Although the change might be "transformational," it is no doubt painful. What I have learned is to be gentler with myself and others as we continue to move through the changes we face, and to affirm the pain while looking for new ways to live hopefully and powerfully.

THE BEAUTY OF A SABBATICAL

After about 15 years in business, I decided to take a sabbatical for a lot of different reasons, including health challenges, feeling burned out with work, and a realization my daughter was growing up way too fast. As a result, I decided to take "3rd Grade" off, and entered a whole new world.

I became a "soccer mom." If you had told me five years earlier I'd enjoy doing this I would have said you were crazy. Here I was, taking care of the house, making dinner, volunteering at school, and shuttling kids to and from dance lessons, girl scouts, and soccer. In addition, I had the luxury of working out at 2:00 in the afternoon, and challenging myself in new ways, such as taking a play-writing class and laying laminate floors. (Since I am not "handy" this was a real stretch!)

The time to decompress and reflect was wonderful. I was lucky to have the opportunity and was courageous enough to take it. The experience changed me. As I headed back to work fifteen months later, I had a renewed sense of who I was, what I enjoy doing, and how I wanted to work. Here are a few things I learned.

- I have value in and of myself, without having to measure up to someone else's standards. I think this is one of the harder lessons to learn in life, especially at work, since we are constantly judged by others whether they are managers, customers, associates, professors, or others. It is easy to become defined by either our latest success or our latest failure. My gift from this time off was a much deeper sense of who I am, which has made me a better consultant—more able to take risks and not take things personally.

- We could live on a lot less money. Cutting our family income for fifteen months forced us to look at how and why we spend money. Despite the loss of income, the stress level in our family went down because our daily routine was much less hectic, and we could spend more time together.

- My low energy level had nothing to do with diet, stress, work, parenting, or disease. I found out I have severe sleep apnea, and, on average, I stopped breathing as many as 40 times per hour. As a result, my brain was not getting enough oxygen, and my body was not getting enough sleep! No wonder I was tired! Had I not had the time and circumstances in which to eliminate all the apparent "stressors" for a period of time, I would not have been as proactive about finding out what was wrong. The good news is I now have a new lease on life, and my old energy level has returned.

- Having a hobby that provides a real, physical payoff helped me balance because I spend so much time in my head.

- I have come to appreciate fine plays not only because of the talent of the actors, but also because the playwright knew how to tell a story, set a mood, and show action simply by dialog. I had a hard time writing meaningful dialog for *several minutes*, let alone hours, so talented playwrights are now among my heroes!

Cathy Perme

Aging Gracefully

"It's not about how old you are, it's about how old you show up."
Teresa Daly, Navigate Forward

My daughter loves to tease me about how old I am, although I don't really feel old. Still, those of us at a "certain age" can't help but be aware of what is going on in our lives and workplaces, as we deal with unprecedented levels of technological and structural change. It goes without saying that the longer you live, the more stuff happens to you. In the last few years, I have counted more than a few colleagues who have retired and know many others who are facing unknown futures. They've decided they are "done," or society has decided for them.

No matter what anyone else says, I know I am not done yet. I am not done learning, I am not done working, I am not done parenting, and I am not done loving. I am not done engaging in life and friend-ships, or sorrow and joy. I am not done writing my book, fixing up my house, or running my business. I love the work I do and the results my clients create for themselves as a result of it. I love learning and applying new things and discovering what is next.

Why do we think we are "done?" Perhaps we tire out; grow out; or burn out of a career, job, or relationship. Perhaps we have stopped learning, or we feel paralyzed by our past successes. Perhaps we are afraid to step into the unknown again and want to play it safe. In complexity theory, that's called "sta-sis," or lack of movement and energy. It's a sure pre-scription for psychological death.

I find I can offer more now than I have ever been able to offer in the past. I'm at the top of my game, having developed a facilitation "praxis" (theory and practice) that is uniquely mine and supports a person-al brand of focus, execution, and results. I've final-ly hit a level of maturity that allows me to weather disappointment and still see the glass as half-full, to know when to double-down on something important and when to let it go, and to care about others without trying to cure them. I do worry others will look at the extra lines on my face, or notice my gimpy knee, and think I am "done." (I've even heard it's a bad idea to acknowledge more than 20 years' experience at anything!) But my role models are successful consultants who are still teaching, facilitating, writing, and learning well into their 70s and 80s. They are having a blast, and they are doing what they love in life.

The reality is most people will have another 20 to 30 years of life *after* age 65, which was unimaginable fewer than 100 years ago. Those extra years are like another lifetime career, folks! For myself at that "certain age" I ask, how do you want to spend that time?

SEVEN SIGNS OF AGELESSNESS

Our culture celebrates youth, but I celebrate people who are ageless. Here are seven characteristics I've observed in people who manage to remain truly ageless:

1. **They relate to people of all ages,** connecting as easily with teens as with octogenarians. They love to find out about people and their lives, and connect on an equal basis.

2. **They know who they are** and don't try to be someone they are not. They seem comfortable in their own skin. They can laugh at themselves and make fun of their own foibles.

3. **They are humble.** Although proud of what they have accomplished in life; they are not defined by it.

4. **They keep learning** and asking "why?" and "how could things be better?" They don't stay stuck in old patterns.

5. **They have found a passion** in their lives and dedicate time to it.

6. **They take care of themselves,** while acknowledging their physical limitations and working around them. They eat well, they rest, and they exercise. They know they aren't invincible.

7. **They are not cynical.** They look for the best in others and they make the *choice* to be happy and engaged in life.

References

(1997). Webster's New World College Dictionary, Fourth Edition. New York, NY: Macmillan USA.

(2004). *Chinese symbol for ox.* Retrieved from https://www.chinese-symbols. com/o-chinese-symbol-for-ox

(2017). Change Solutions for Organizations. Retrieved from https://www.human-synergistics.com/change-solutions/ change-solutions-for-organizations

(2017). Human Systems Dynamics Institute. Retrieved from https://www.hsdinstitute.org

Beckhard, R. & Harris, R. T.   Organizational
      Transitions: Managing Complex Change (2nd
      Ed.) Reading, MA: Addison-Wesley.

Confucius quotes: Translation, introduction, and an-
      notation copyright © 2014 by David Hinton,
      from *Analects.* Reprinted by permission of
      Counterpoint.

Cooke, R. & Lafferty, J. (2011). *Culture Makes*
      the Difference in the Business Objects and
      Crystal Decisions Merger. Retrieved from
      https://www.humansynergistics.com/re-
      sources/content/2017/05/15/culture-makes-
      the-difference-in-the-business-objects-and-
      crystal-decisions-merger

Fritz, R. (1984, 1989). The Path of Least Resis-
      tance: Learning to Become the Creative
      Force in Your Own Life. Walpole, NH:
      Stillpoint Publishing.

Fritz, R. (1991). Creating: A Practical Guide to
      the Creative Process and How to Use It to
      Create Anything—a Work of Art, a Relation-
      ship, a Career or a Better Life. New York,
      NY: Fawcett Columbine.

Gladwell, M. (2008). Outliers: The Story of Success. New York, NY: Little, Brown and Company.

Human Systems Dynamics Institute. (2016, May 13). *Simple Rules.* Retrieved from http://www.hsdinstitute.org/resources/simple-rules.html

Jones, Q., Dunphy, D., Fishman, R., Larne-Jones, M., & Canter, C. (2006). In Great Company: Unlocking the Secrets of Cultural Transformation. Mount Prospect, IL: Human Synergistics International.

Kliesen Wehrman, C. (1994). 8 basic rules of improvisation [Class handout]. Dudley Riggs Brave New Workshop, Minneapolis, Minnesota.

Kotter, J. P., & Heskett, J. L. (1992). Corporate Culture and Performance. New York, NY: The Free Press.

O'Neill, J. (1993, 2004). The Paradox of Success: When Winning at Work Means Losing at Life. New York, NY: G. P. Putnam's Sons.

Peck, M. Scott. (1978). The Road Less Traveled. New York, NY: Simon & Schuster.

Schein, E.H. (1999). The Corporate Culture Survival Guide. San Francisco, CA: Jossey-Bass.

Senge, P. M. (2006). The Fifth Discipline: The Art and Practice of the Learning Organization. New York, NY: Doubleday/Currency.

Simple Rules. (2017, September 17). Retrieved from http://www.hsdinstitute.org/assets/documents/5.1.1.14-simple-rules-14may16.pdf

Trust. (2017). In Merriam-Webster.com. Retrieved September 30, 2017, from https://www.merriam-webster.com/dictionary/trust

ENDNOTES

1 This essay was written with Anne Knapp, former COO and CEO, who helped her organizations weather a great deal of turbulence over time!

2 Human Systems Dynamics Institute – www. Hsdinstitute.org

3 Includes research conducted by John Kotter for his book, Corporate Culture and Performance from 1987-1991 (as listed in References) and much research conducted by Human Synergistics, Inc. www.humansynergistics.com

4 This essay was authored with Larry Hofschulte, with whom I worked to develop teams to improve quality and redesign work processes.

5 This essay was written with Glenda Eoyang, founder of the field of Human Systems Dynamics and an incredibly empowering leader herself.

6   I learned this approach from Larry Porter (University Associates) in a group facilitation workshop.

7   Written by Chris Kliesen Wehrman (1994), adapted and reprinted with permission

8   Excerpt(s) from THE PARADOX OF SUCCESS: WHEN WINNING AT WORK MEANS LOSING AT LIFE by John R. O'Neil, copyright © 1993 by John O'Neil. Used by permission of Tarcher, an imprint of Penguin Publishing Group, a division of Penguin Random House LLC. All rights reserved.

9   "Creative Tension" is a concept and theory developed by Robert Fritz in his books The Path of Least Resistance and Creating. Peter Senge further discusses it in The Fifth Discipline.

10   My thanks to Patricia Schuckert for planting these ideas. Her business focuses on helping people integrate body, mind, and spirit for effective work and life.

About the Author

Catherine M. (Cathy) Perme is a change agent with deep experience in organizational change, who has also been changed personally!

Cathy's background includes nearly thirty years of experience in organizational consulting as the owner and president of a regional consulting firm headquartered in Minneapolis, MN. Her firm, C. M. Perme & Associates LLC, has helped hundreds of organizations, from two-person firms to multinational corporations, to focus clearly, organize effectively, and act with courage. She enjoys working with all levels of an organization, from line workers to CEO's. She believes that we all have the opportunity to "take the lead" in both our professional and personal lives and offers practical advice on how to do that, as well as when to back off and why.

Adopting her daughter, Lucy, has been the most meaningful experience in all walks of her life. Watching her daughter grow up and become her own person has been fun, challenging, crazy-making, and proud. And she would not have changed one thing!